# my first book of questions and answers

# cars

## James Pickering

This is a Parragon Book
First published in 2002

Parragon
Queen Street House
4 Queen Street
Bath BA1 1HE, UK

Copyright © Parragon 2002

*Produced by*

David West 🏃 Children's Books
7 Princeton Court
55 Felsham Road
Putney
London SW15 1AZ

British Library Cataloguing-in-Publication Data

A catalogue record for this book is available from
the British Library.

ISBN 0-75258-456-1

Printed in China

*Designers*
Axis Design, Aarti Parmar, Rob Shone,
Fiona Thorne

*Illustrators*
Mike Lacey, Dud Moseley (SGA)

*Cartoonist*
Peter Wilks (SGA)

*Editor*
Ross McLaughness

# CONTENTS

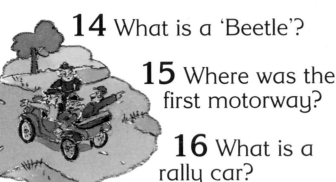
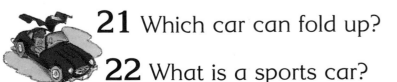

# How did people travel before cars?

Before cars were invented, people often travelled in wheeled carriages, pulled by teams of horses. The journey was dusty, uncomfortable and usually quite slow.

Early steam car

# Did cars run on steam?

Several early cars ran on steam power, just like steam trains. Steam engines were more powerful than petrol engines, but they were very heavy and it was hard work to keep them running.

# What fuel do cars use?

For over 100 years, most cars have run on petrol. At first there were very few petrol stations, so most drivers carried cans of spare fuel with them. Cars with petrol engines run more quickly than cars with steam engines.

Early petrol station

## ❓ What was the first car?

The first car to be sold was the three-wheeled Benz Patent Motorwagen, in 1887. It looked more like a chair on wheels than a car, and was so slow that it couldn't travel up hills!

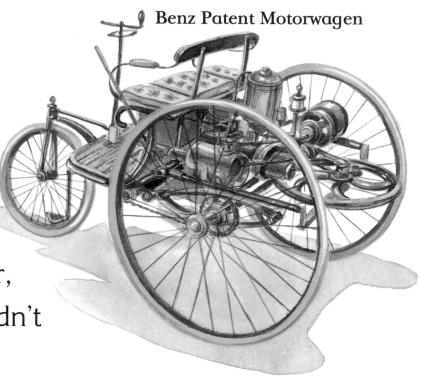

Benz Patent Motorwagen

## ❓ How were early cars steered?

Early cars didn't have steering wheels. Instead, drivers steered with a lever, or by turning handles on a small wheel at the end of a pole.

# ❓ *Who was Daimler?*

Gottlieb Daimler was a German engineer, who built the first ever motorcycle in 1885. He also built one of the first four-wheeled petrol driven cars. Daimler's cars were very difficult to drive, but they worked much better than other early cars.

Daimler's first car

# When was the first car race?

The first car race was in 1894, between Paris and Rouen in France – 13 cars took part. The fastest was a huge de Dion steam tractor, which travelled at less than 19 kph.

Early car race

# What was a 'Blower Bentley'?

'Blower Bentleys' were very fast racing cars in the 1920s and 1930s. They were fitted with a blower, or supercharger, which drove extra fuel into the engine to make the car super-quick.

Blower Bentley

# Which car was never happy?

Camille Jenatzy's electric car was called 'La Jamais Contente', ('never happy' in French). But Jenatzy was happy, when the car broke the world speed record.

'La Jamais Contente'

## Which car was a baby?

The Austin Seven was nicknamed the 'baby Austin' because it was so tiny. Four people could only just fit inside it, but it became Britain's most popular car in the 1920s.

Austin Seven

## Which cars only came in black?

The Model 'T' Ford, or 'Tin Lizzie', always left the factory painted black. In its day, the Model 'T' was the most popular car in the world. Over 15 million were built!

Model 'T' Ford

Charabanc

# ? *Which car travelled to the seaside?*

Charabancs were the first motorised coaches. Groups of friends used to hire long charabancs for special trips to the seaside or to the city. The passengers sat on wooden benches behind the driver.

## ❓ *Which car was the most comfortable?*

Rolls Royces are very quiet, comfortable and expensive cars. The 1907 Silver Ghost was no exception. Owners rarely drove themselves, but preferred to relax in the back!

Rolls Royce Silver Ghost

## ❓ *Which car was 'royal'?*

Ettore Bugatti hoped that every royal family in Europe would buy a Bugatti Royale, but only six were ever built. Today, each one is worth millions of pounds.

Bugatti Royale

# ? *What was a Cord?*

The Cord was one of the most comfortable American cars of the 1920s and 1930s, but they were very expensive, and very few were built. Luckily, many of them still exist.

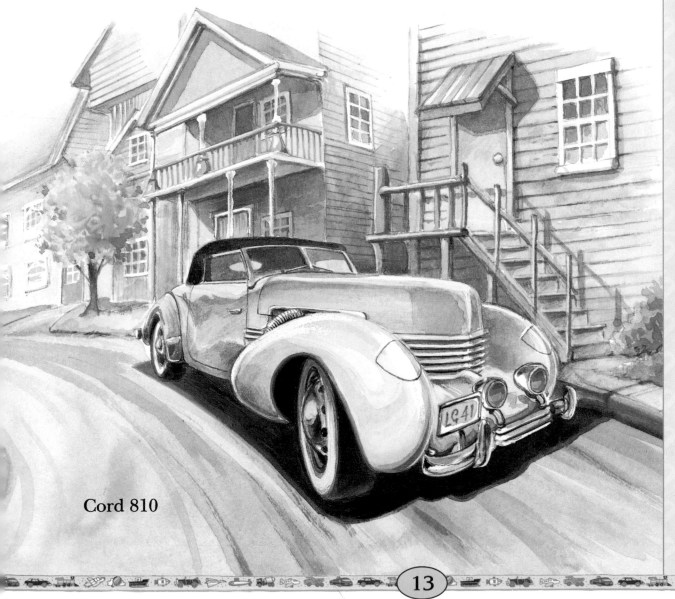

Cord 810

# ? Who built big family cars?

American cars were always much bigger than European cars. Their roads were wider, and petrol was also cheaper than in Europe, which meant that many American families could afford to run a large family car.

1939 Plymouth

# ? What is a 'Beetle'?

The first Volkswagen was nicknamed the 'Beetle' or 'Bug' because it looks a bit like an insect. Over 40 million have been made since 1938.

# ? *Where was the first motorway?*

Before cars were invented, most roads were narrow and bumpy. As cars became faster, bigger roads were needed. The first motorway was built in Germany in 1921.

Volkswagen Beetles

**Beetles are able to swim.**

**TRUE**. During World War Two, the German army built a special Volkswagen Beetle, which could travel through rivers.

**Motorists often lost their way.**

**TRUE**. There used to be very few road signs, so it was difficult to find your way. Sensible motorists carried maps in their cars.

# ❓ What is a rally car?

❓ Rally cars are family cars, which have been given extra-powerful engines for off-road racing. Rally cars skid across country, through mud, snow and across ice. Accidents often happen, and drivers are protected by crash helmets and safety harnesses.

# ❓ What is Formula One?

Formula One racing takes place around the world every year. Formula One cars have very powerful engines and huge fins, which stop the cars from taking off at high speed!

Formula One racing car

Rally car

# ? How fast can racing cars go?

Formula One cars race at speeds of over 250 kph, but American Indycar racing is faster. Indycars can zoom along at 375 kph – that's over four times faster than the speed limit on American motorways.

Indycar racer

All races are very short.

**FALSE.** Dragster races only last for a few seconds, but the Le Mans race in France lasts for 24 hours – a whole day and night!

Cars race through cities.

**TRUE.** Formula One races take place in cities in Monaco and Australia, but the streets are cleared of traffic and people before the race.

# Which cars had fins?

Oldsmobile

During the 1950s, many colourful American cars, such as Oldsmobiles, had huge fins, shiny metal bumpers and bright lights fitted to them. Some of them looked more like alien spaceships than cars!

# Which cars are stretched?

Stretched limousine

Limousines can be stretched, so that they are as long as a train. The longest limousine in the world had 26 wheels, a swimming pool, a bed and a helicopter landing pad! It was 30.5 m long – about ten times longer than a family car.

Tucker '48

## ❓ *Which car was a goose?*

The Tucker '48 was an unusual car, nicknamed the 'Tin Goose'. The engine was at the back of the car, and its front headlight swivelled as the driver turned the steering wheel.

## Who travelled in a bubble?

The BMW Isetta was nicknamed the 'bubble car' because of its shape. These tiny three-wheelers only had one door, at the front. There was only room for the driver and one passenger.

BMW Isetta 'bubble car'

## Which car is smart?

Smart Car

The Smart Car is a very small modern car which is perfect for nipping around crowded cities. Because it's so short and slim, the Smart Car takes up very little room when it's not being used – drivers can park it sideways against the pavement.

Renault Zoom concept car

**?** *Which car can fold up?*

**?** The Renault Zoom can fold up its back wheels to make itself shorter, so that it can park in small spaces. It also has an electric motor, instead of a petrol engine, and doesn't make lots of dirty fumes like other cars.

# ? What is a sports car?

Ferrari F40

Sports cars are meant to be driven for fun. Often they have a fold-down roof, a small boot, and they're usually much faster than ordinary cars.

# ? Which car is named after a snake?

The AC Cobra is named after a poisonous snake. These cars have massive engines, fat tyres and extra-strong bodies for driving at high speed. Cobras make superb racing cars.

AC Cobra

# ? *What is a muscle car?*

Muscle cars are ordinary cars which have been souped-up for high performance. The Shelby Mustang was a Ford Mustang, specially tuned by racing driver Carroll Shelby.

Shelby Mustang

# What was an Aerocar?

The Aerocar was a car which could really fly. When it was driving on the road, the Aerocar folded up its wings and tail.

Aerocar

# Which car could dive underwater?

James Bond's
Lotus Esprit

In the film The Spy Who Loved Me, James Bond's Lotus sports car could turn into a submarine and swim underwater. People got a shock when they saw it driving out of the water on to a beach!

# ❓ *What is a hot rod?*

A hot rod is an old family car which has been given an extra-powerful engine, a lowered roof, huge tyres and a colourful paint job. Hot rods are raced all over the world.

Hot rods

## TRUE OR FALSE?

**Some cars are funny.**

**TRUE.** Funny cars are family cars with stretched bodies and huge engines which take part in dragster races.

**All cars are made in factories.**

**FALSE.** Some sports cars can be bought in kit form, to be built at home just like a model aeroplane, only much bigger!

# What is a dragster?

A dragster is a very powerful racing car, which races along a short track at enormous speed. Dragsters are so fast that brakes alone can't stop them – they also need parachutes to slow them down.

Thrust SSC

Dragster

# What's the fastest car ever?

Thrust SSC was the first car to travel faster than the speed of sound, in 1997. Thrust had four parachutes and two massive jet engines, which are normally used to power fighter aircraft!

Bluebird

# Which bird travelled at 484 kph?

Malcolm Campbell broke the land speed record nine times in his Bluebird cars during the 1930s. 484 kph is about twice as fast as a modern sports car can travel.

## Which car could drive itself?

KITT was the name of a special car in the television series Knightrider. KITT could drive on its own, and could even talk to its owner, to warn him if he was being followed by baddies!

KITT

## What was Chitty Chitty Bang Bang?

Chitty Chitty Bang Bang

Only three Chitty Chitty Bang Bang cars were built. They had huge, powerful plane engines, and won many races, even though they were difficult to drive and hardly had any brakes.

# Which car had an ejector seat?

James Bond's Aston Martin DB5 had an ejector seat. When he wanted to get rid of someone, Bond pressed a button, the roof opened, and his passenger was shot into the air!

Aston Martin DB5

# ❓ What was Sunraycer?

Every year, there's a race in Australia for cars which use sunshine for fuel. Sunraycer was an unusual-looking car which crossed the country at a speed of about 40 kph. Luckily, there's plenty of sunshine in Australia!

Sunraycer

# ? Which car fits in a suitcase?

This strange Japanese compact car is so small, that it can fit into a suitcase. At the end of the journey, the case folds up, and the driver can carry the car away.

# ? How fast can electric cars travel?

Electric cars are usually slower than petrol-driven cars, but one electric three-wheeler called Alien was said to have reached 240 kph – as fast as a modern sports car.

Alien

## TRUE OR FALSE?

**Some cars have sails.**

**TRUE.** Sand yachts are sailing boats on wheels. The wind in their sails can push these three-wheelers to 125 kph.

**Some electric cars use petrol.**

**TRUE.** Combination cars are electric cars with a petrol generator. The generator charges the electric batteries, which give power to the car.

# Index